Lila and Andy learn

I0151673

What happens when you Flush!

How Wastewater gets clean again

Revised & Updated Second Edition

Kenneth Adams

Copyright © 2025 by Kenneth Adams
All rights reserved.

No portion of this book may be reproduced in any form without written permission from the publisher or author, except as permitted by copyright law. This publication is designed to provide general information in regard to the subject matter covered. It is sold with the understanding that neither the author nor the publisher is engaged in rendering any professional services. While the publisher or author have used their best efforts in preparing this book, they make no representations or warranties with respect to the accuracy or completeness of the contents of this book and specifically disclaim any implied warranties of fitness for a particular purpose.

Book Cover by Kenneth Adams
Illustrations and Images by Kenneth Adams
Illustrations and Images created with AI Assistance
Second Edition 2025

ISBN: 978-1-998552-30-6

Water is critical to life on Earth.
Always be responsible. Conserve water today to
preserve life tomorrow.

This book belongs to:

_____

Hi, I'm Lila. One of my absolute favorite hobbies is knitting and crocheting! I know, you may think that's only for old people, but I just love turning colorful yarn into cozy creations.

Whether it's a new, fun scarf for Mom or a multi-colored bucket hat for Dad, there's always something new I'm working on.

I have a brother, Andy, and we love each other's company. We always find exciting ways to spend our time and make every day an adventure.

Hey, I'm Andy, Lila's brother.
I'm very curious to know what your passion is. What is the thing you do that makes you the happiest?

For me, it's sketching. I always make sure to have my sketchbook or tablet nearby, and I don't even care where I start. I just doodle a couple of lines and then let my imagination run wild.

Together with Lila, I'm always out and about, discovering new things and places. This way we learn and grow our minds, while I also find inspiration for my artwork.

Have you ever wondered what happens with water that goes down the drain after you take a shower or flush the toilet? Well, wonder no more! We're about to go on an epic journey of discovery to learn all about the process of cleaning dirty water!

Since water is such an important part of our life, and because water is so scarce in many areas of the world, engineers and scientists have developed ways to clean dirty water before allowing it to flow back into nature.

Water that drains away after being used is called __wastewater__ or __sewage__. Wastewater may also include household stuff like leftover food scraps, soaps, and oils. Basically, everything that you drain with the water will come along for the ride.

Wastewater also does not only come from our houses. Anywhere water is used, wastewater is created. This includes big factories, restaurants, hospitals, and schools. Even places where we go for fun, like adventure and water parks, produce wastewater.

Once water flows down the drain in your house, it collects in an underground pipe, called a <u>sewer pipe</u>. The sewer pipe from your house connects with the sewer pipes from other houses to form an underground network of sewerage pipes, collecting all the sewage together.

The more wastewater they collect, the bigger the pipes become. The sewer pipes then carry all the collected sewage to a special place called a <u>wastewater treatment plant</u>.

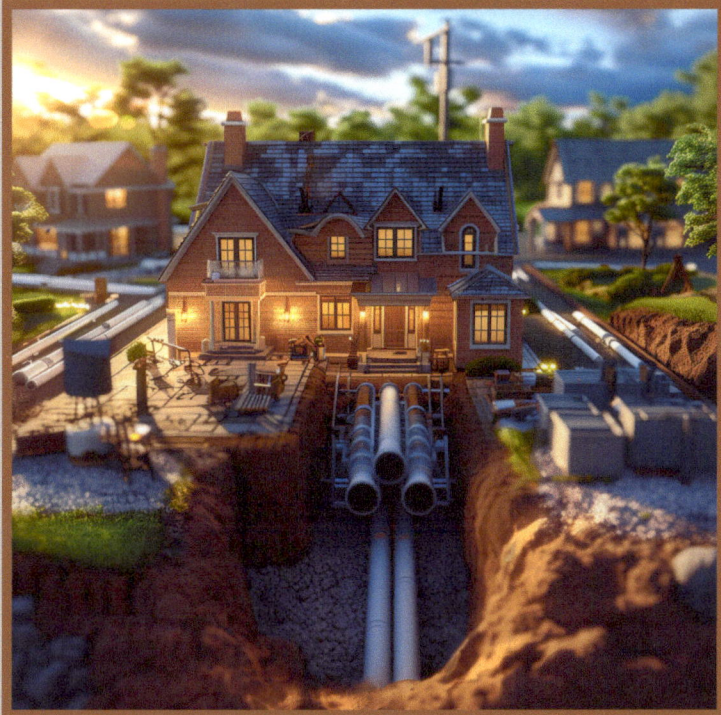

Wastewater from our homes flow into underground sewer pipes

Sewer pipes from our homes collect into bigger pipes

On its way to the wastewater treatment plant, gravity helps the water flow through the sewer pipes. Sometimes the water has to travel quite far before reaching the treatment plant, and gravity may not be enough to make the water flow fast enough. That's when pump stations are helpful.

Inside a pump station, special equipment called pumps are installed to "push" the wastewater along the sewer pipes.

Pump stations are also sometimes called lift stations, because the pumps "lift" the wastewater, making sure it flows through the pipes fast enough so it doesn't block the pipes, especially if the water has to travel uphill.

Finally, the wastewater reaches the <u>wastewater treatment plant</u>. A wastewater treatment plant is the facility where wastewater is cleaned.

Wastewater treatment plants come in all sizes, depending on how much sewage they need to clean.

It is the job of a <u>Civil Engineer</u> to determine how big the treatment plant has to be to clean all the sewage a town or city may produce.

Cleaning wastewater involves a number of steps. The steps are divided into two main categories, Primary Treatment and Secondary Treatment.

During primary treatment, all the large, unwanted, solid floating items are removed from the wastewater.

After taking out all the big stuff, it's then time for the secondary treatment. This process gets rid of the tiniest leftover bits we don't want, making the water even cleaner.

Large, chunky items like plastics and toys are removed during Primary Treatment

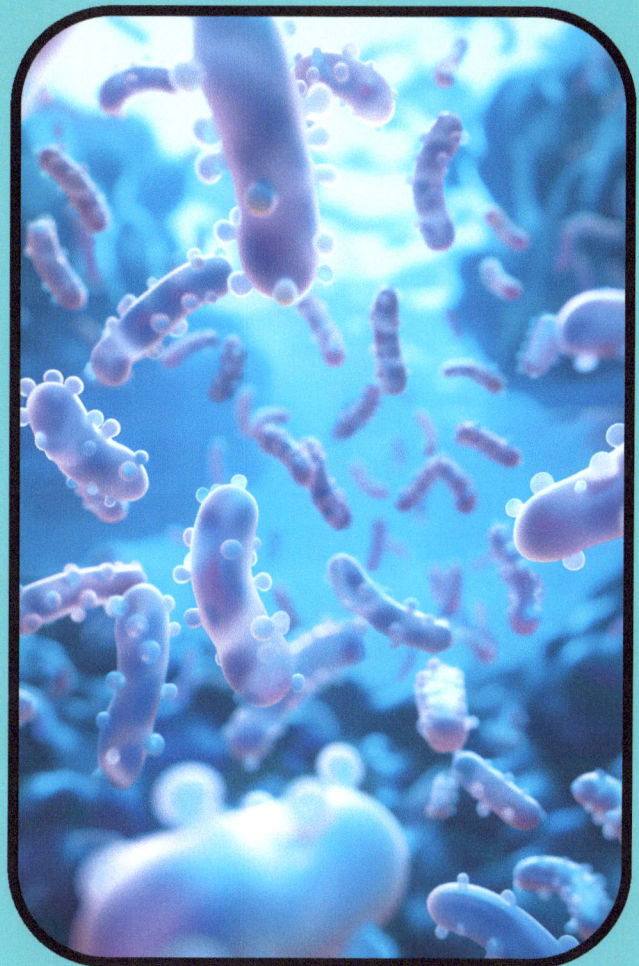

Tiny items like food scraps and bacteria are removed during Secondary Treatment

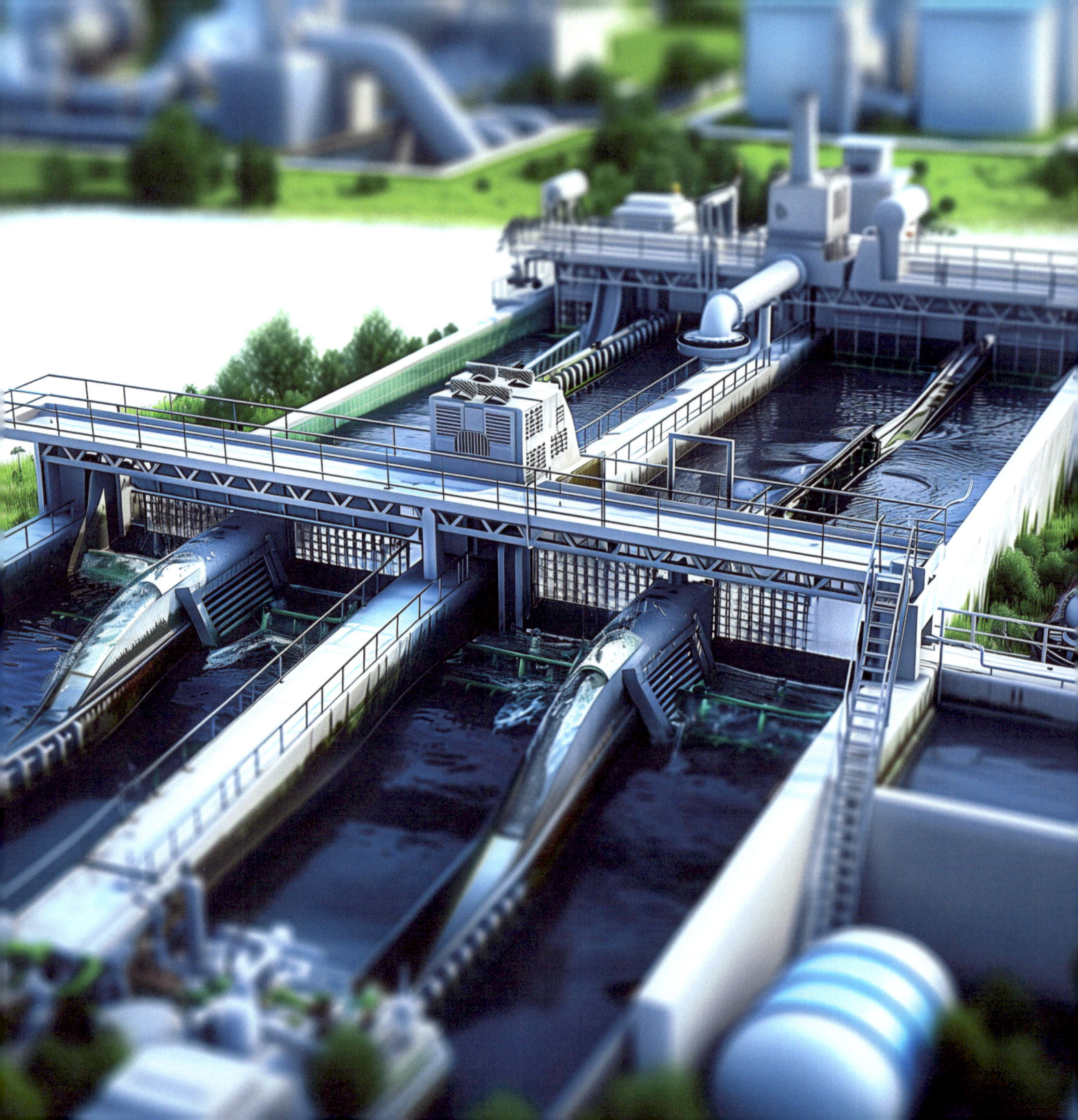

The Wastewater Treatment Process

Primary Treatment
Step 1: Screening

The first step of the primary treatment process is <u>screening</u>, where the wastewater is made to flow through giant screens. A screen is a special piece of equipment that looks like a metal grid. It works like a giant strainer by trapping all the big items like toys, clothing, or plastics, while allowing the water to flow through.

Even though big items can be removed from the water at the treatment plant, it is important to remember not to flush large things down the drain or the toilet, as they may clog the pipes or damage equipment such as pumps that help the water flow.

The Wastewater Treatment Process

Primary Treatment
Step 2: Grit Removal

After screening is complete and all the big items have been removed, the wastewater still contains heavy materials like sand, gravel, and pebbles. These materials are called grit, and to remove them, the water flows through a <u>grit removal</u> tank.

Since sand and pebbles are heavier than water, they sink to the bottom of the grit removal tank due to gravity. The grit can then be removed from the bottom of the tank, while the water exits the tank at the top.

Grit Removal

Water flows in →

Water flows out →

Grit falls to the bottom of the tank.

Grit settles at the bottom of the tank, where it can be removed.

The Wastewater Treatment Process

Primary Treatment

Step 3: Primary Clarification

The final step of the primary treatment process is called <u>Primary Clarification</u>.

After the grit has been removed from the wastewater, it flows into a large settling tank, where heavier solids like coffee grounds and other non-living things sink to the bottom to form <u>sludge</u>, while lighter materials like fats, oils, and grease float to the surface to form <u>scum</u>.

Since they are now separated, the sludge and scum are then easily removed from the wastewater.

The sludge that gets removed during treatment doesn't go to waste. After further processing, much of it can be turned into fertilizer to help plants grow, or it can be safely disposed of in special landfills designed for this purpose.

Scum rises to the top of the tank

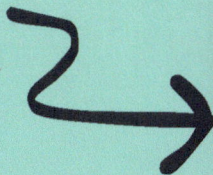

Sludge sinks to the bottom of the tank

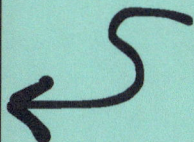

The Wastewater Treatment Process

Up to this point, all the big, chunky items, the grit and the fats, oils, and grease have been removed from the wastewater. It's now time for Secondary Treatment to happen.

Secondary Treatment
Step 1: Aeration

The first step of the secondary treatment process is called aeration. The wastewater flows into big aeration tanks, where oxygen is added to the water, like a big bubble bath. The oxygen in the water allows helpful bacteria to grow. Bacteria are living organisms, like tiny little bugs, that eat away all the leftover food scraps and other small things that are still present in the water.

During aeration, oxygen is added by blowing air into the wastewater.

The Wastewater Treatment Process

Secondary Treatment
Step 2: Secondary Clarification

After the bacteria did their job by eating all the food and other living waste, the water enters another settling tank called the <u>Secondary Clarification Tank</u>.

In this tank, the remaining sludge, which now includes the bacteria, sinks to the bottom and is separated from the treated water.

The Wastewater Treatment Process

Secondary Treatment
Step 3: Disinfection

After the water has been cleaned through primary and secondary treatment, it's time for one final important step, <u>disinfection</u>. This process kills any harmful germs, bacteria, or viruses that might still be hiding in the water.

Treatment plants often use chlorine, like what's used to clean swimming pools, or special ultraviolet lights to make sure the water is completely safe. This step is crucial to protect both people and the environment.

Once the wastewater has been thoroughly cleaned, the water is tested to make sure it's ready to go back to nature.

Testing is when a team of engineers and scientists checks the water with special tools to search for any tiny germs that might still be hiding in the water. If it passes all the tests, the treated wastewater is released back into a river, stream, lake, or even the ocean.

If, however, the water is still not clean enough to return to nature, the water treatment plant can also conduct additional treatment until it passes all the tests, and the water is clean enough to be released.

Now you know how the dirty water that drains from our homes, schools, and businesses is cleaned.

By cleaning wastewater and then putting it back into nature to be used again, we save precious, clean water for drinking, swimming, and all sorts of fun! The clean water that goes back into rivers and lakes eventually becomes part of the water cycle again. Rain falls, rivers flow, and that same water might end up back in our taps as drinking water someday!

This amazing process helps the same water get used over and over again, making it the ultimate recycling process.

Careers in Wastewater Treatment

If you care about protecting the environment and keeping our communities healthy by cleaning the water we use every day, then careers dedicated to wastewater treatment might be perfect for you! There are many exciting jobs for people who want to help create the systems that turn dirty water back into clean water that can safely return to nature. Here are examples of careers that work together to clean every drop of wastewater before it goes back to our rivers, lakes, and oceans.

Engineering & Design:

- <u>Civil Engineer</u> - Designs wastewater treatment plants, sewer systems, and pipe networks. They figure out how big plants need to be and where pipes should go.

- <u>Environmental Engineer</u> - Specializes in creating systems that protect the environment, including advanced water treatment technologies.

- <u>Process Engineer</u> - Designs the specific steps and equipment used to clean wastewater, making sure each treatment process works efficiently.

- <u>Hydraulic Engineer</u> - Focuses on how water flows through pipes and treatment systems, ensuring proper water movement and pressure.

- <u>Chemical Engineer</u> - Develops chemical processes used in water treatment and designs systems for adding chemicals safely.

Operations & Maintenance:

- <u>Wastewater Treatment Plant Operator</u> - Runs the day-to-day operations of treatment plants, monitoring equipment and making sure water gets cleaned properly.

- <u>Water Quality Technician</u> - Tests water samples throughout the treatment process to make sure it meets safety standards.

- <u>Equipment Maintenance Technician</u> - Repairs and maintains pumps, motors, pipes, and other equipment that keeps treatment plants running.

- <u>Instrumentation Technician</u> - Maintains and calibrates the electronic sensors and computer systems that monitor treatment processes.

Laboratory and Testing:

- <u>Laboratory Analyst</u> - Tests water samples for bacteria, chemicals, and other substances to ensure treatment is working correctly.

- <u>Microbiologist</u> - Studies the bacteria and other microorganisms used in wastewater treatment to help optimize biological processes.

- <u>Water Quality Specialist</u> - Monitors treated water to ensure it meets environmental standards before being released.

Regulatory and Compliance:

- <u>Environmental Compliance Officer</u> - Makes sure wastewater treatment plants follow all environmental laws and regulations.

- <u>Water Resource Manager</u> - Plans how communities will manage their water resources, including wastewater treatment capacity.

- <u>Environmental Inspector</u> - Visits treatment plants to check that they're operating according to environmental regulations.

Research and Development:

- <u>Water Treatment Researcher</u> - Develops new technologies and methods for cleaning wastewater more effectively.

- <u>Environmental Scientist</u> - Studies the effects of wastewater discharge on the environment and develops better protection methods.

- <u>Process Development Engineer</u> - Creates and tests new treatment processes to make wastewater cleaning more efficient.

Wastewater Treatment Glossary

A <u>glossary</u> is like a mini-dictionary of terms with definitions.

Here's a glossary of terms associated with <u>Wastewater Treatment</u>.

<u>Activated Sludge</u> - A mixture of helpful bacteria and other tiny organisms that eat waste in wastewater. It's called "activated" because the bacteria are very active and hungry!

<u>Aeration</u> - The process of adding oxygen to water, like creating a giant bubble bath. This helps bacteria grow so they can eat the waste in the water.

<u>Bacteria</u> - Tiny living organisms, like microscopic bugs, that eat waste and help clean water. Most bacteria in wastewater treatment are helpful and do important work.

<u>Biosolids</u> - The cleaned and processed sludge that comes from wastewater treatment. It can be used as fertilizer to help plants grow.

<u>Blackwater</u> - Wastewater from toilets that contains human waste. This type of water needs special treatment because it has more germs.

<u>Chlorine</u> - A chemical used to kill harmful germs in water. It's similar to what's used in swimming pools, but in much smaller amounts.

<u>Civil Engineer</u> - A type of engineer who designs and builds things like wastewater treatment plants, bridges, and roads to help communities.

<u>Clarifier</u> - Another name for a settling tank where heavy particles sink to the bottom and lighter materials float to the top.

<u>Coagulation</u> - A process where special chemicals are added to water to make tiny particles stick together into bigger clumps that are easier to remove.

<u>Disinfection</u> - The final step in water treatment that kills any remaining harmful germs, bacteria, or viruses to make the water safe.

<u>Dissolved Oxygen</u> - The amount of oxygen mixed into water. Fish and other water creatures need dissolved oxygen to breathe, and helpful bacteria need it to do their cleaning work.

<u>Effluent</u> - The clean water that flows out of a wastewater treatment plant after all the cleaning steps are finished.

<u>Filtration</u> - Passing water through special materials like sand, gravel, or fabric to trap tiny particles and make the water cleaner.

<u>Flocculation</u> - After coagulation, this process gently mixes the water so the stuck-together particles form even bigger clumps that settle out more easily.

<u>Greywater</u> - Wastewater from sinks, showers, and washing machines. It's called "grey" because it's not as dirty as blackwater from toilets.

<u>Grit</u> - Heavy materials like sand, gravel, and small pebbles that get into wastewater and need to be removed so they don't damage equipment.

<u>Influent</u> - The dirty wastewater that flows into a treatment plant before any cleaning has been done.

<u>Lagoon</u> - A type of wastewater treatment that uses large, shallow ponds where bacteria naturally clean the water over several months.

<u>Lift Station</u> - Another name for a pump station. It "lifts" wastewater to higher levels when gravity alone can't move it through the pipes.

<u>Nitrogen</u> - A nutrient found in wastewater that can be harmful to rivers and lakes if not removed. Treatment plants have special ways to take it out.

<u>Outfall</u> - The pipe or opening where clean, treated water flows back into a river, lake, or ocean.

<u>Pathogen</u> - Harmful germs, bacteria, or viruses that can make people and animals sick. Wastewater treatment removes these dangerous organisms.

<u>pH</u> - A measure of how acidic or basic water is. Wastewater treatment plants monitor pH to make sure the water is safe for the environment.

<u>Phosphorus</u> - Another nutrient in wastewater that can cause problems in rivers and lakes by making too much algae grow. Treatment plants work to remove it.

<u>Primary Clarification</u> - A settling tank where heavier solids sink to the bottom to form sludge, while lighter materials like oils float to the top as scum.

<u>Primary Treatment</u> - The first main stage of cleaning wastewater, where big items, grit, and floating materials are removed.

Pump Station - A facility with special pumps that push wastewater through sewer pipes when gravity isn't strong enough to move it.

Screening - The first step in wastewater treatment where large objects are caught by metal grids that work like giant strainers.

Scum - Light materials like fats, oils, and grease that float to the surface of settling tanks and get skimmed off.

Secondary Clarification - A settling tank used after the aeration process where bacteria and remaining particles sink to the bottom.

Secondary Treatment - The second main stage of cleaning wastewater, where bacteria eat the remaining waste and make the water much cleaner.

Sewage - Another word for wastewater. All the used water and waste that goes down drains and toilets.

Sewer Pipe - Underground pipes that carry wastewater from homes and businesses to the treatment plant.

Sludge - The thick mixture of solids that settles to the bottom of treatment tanks. After processing, it can become useful biosolids.

Suspended Solids - Tiny particles floating in water that make it look cloudy or dirty. Treatment removes these to make the water clear.

Tertiary Treatment - An extra level of cleaning beyond primary and secondary treatment, used when water needs to be extra clean.

Ultraviolet (UV) Light - Special invisible light that kills germs and bacteria. It's used as a chemical-free way to disinfect water.

Wastewater - Used water from homes, schools, businesses, and factories that contains waste and needs to be cleaned before going back to nature.

Wastewater Treatment Plant - A facility where dirty water is cleaned through many steps before being safely returned to rivers, lakes, or oceans.

Water Cycle - The natural process where water moves from the earth to the sky and back again through evaporation, rain, and flowing in rivers and streams.

What Happens When You Flush

Quiz

Multiple Choice (Choose the best answer)

1. What is wastewater also called?
   a) Greywater
   b) Sewage
   c) Effluent
   d) Influent

2. What helps water flow through sewer pipes?
   a) Pumps only
   b) Pressure
   c) Gravity
   d) Chemicals

3. What is the first step in primary treatment?
   a) Grit removal
   b) Screening
   c) Primary clarification
   d) Aeration

4. What are the tiny organisms that eat waste in wastewater called?
   a) Bacteria
   b) Algae
   c) Fish
   d) Viruses

5. What do pump stations do?
   a) Clean the water
   b) Test the water
   c) Push wastewater through pipes
   d) Add chemicals

6. What forms when lighter materials float to the surface?
   a) Sludge
   b) Grit
   c) Scum
   d) Biosolids

7. What is added during the aeration process?
   a) Chlorine
   b) Bacteria
   c) Chemicals
   d) Oxygen

8. What kills harmful germs in the disinfection step?
   a) Bacteria and oxygen
   b) Chlorine or UV light
   c) Sludge and scum
   d) Grit and sand

9. Who determines how big a treatment plant needs to be?
   a) Water Quality Technician
   b) Laboratory Analyst
   c) Civil Engineer
   d) Plant Operator

10. What are heavy materials like sand and pebbles called?
    a) Scum
    b) Sludge
    c) Biosolids
    d) Grit

11. What can processed sludge be turned into?
    a) Drinking water
    b) Fertilizer
    c) Fuel
    d) Plastic

12. What is wastewater from toilets called?
    a) Greywater
    b) Influent
    c) Blackwater
    d) Effluent

13. Where does clean treated water go?
    a) Back to homes
    b) Storage tanks
    c) Rivers, lakes, or oceans
    d) Underground pipes

14. What are pump stations also called?
    a) Screening stations
    b) Lift stations
    c) Clarification stations
    d) Aeration stations

15. What is the clean water leaving a treatment plant called?
    a) Influent
    b) Sewage
    c) Wastewater
    d) Effluent

16. What type of engineer specializes in environmental protection?
    a) Civil Engineer
    b) Environmental Engineer
    c) Process Engineer
    d) Chemical Engineer

17. Who tests water samples throughout treatment?
    a) Civil Engineer
    b) Plant Operator
    c) Water Quality Technician
    d) Maintenance Technician

18. What connects houses to the sewer network?
    a) Lift stations
    b) Sewer pipes
    c) Pump stations
    d) Treatment plants

19. What happens during secondary clarification?
    a) Oxygen is added
    b) Large items are removed
    c) Bacteria and particles sink
    d) Water is disinfected

20. What do bacteria need to grow and work effectively?
    a) Heat
    b) Oxygen
    c) Chemicals
    d) Light

21. What measures how acidic or basic water is?
    a) Temperature
    b) Dissolved oxygen
    c) pH
    d) Turbidity

22. What can cause too much algae to grow in lakes?
    a) Oxygen
    b) Chlorine
    c) Phosphorus
    d) Bacteria

23. Who runs day-to-day plant operations?
    a) Civil Engineer
    b) Environmental Inspector
    c) Laboratory Analyst
    d) Plant Operator

24. What is the mixture of helpful bacteria called?
    a) Biosolids
    b) Activated sludge
    c) Scum
    d) Grit

25. What invisible light kills germs without chemicals?
    a) Infrared light
    b) Visible light
    c) Ultraviolet light
    d) Fluorescent light

Fill-in-the-Blank

26. Water that drains away after being used is called _____ or sewage.

27. The underground pipes that carry wastewater are called _____ pipes.

28. The first step of primary treatment is _____, where large objects are trapped.

29. Heavy materials like sand and pebbles are called _____.

30. The process of adding oxygen to water is called _____.

31. Light materials that float to the surface form _____.

32. The thick mixture that settles to the bottom is called _____.

33. Tiny living organisms that eat waste are called _____.

34. The final step that kills harmful germs is called _____.

35. A _____ engineer designs wastewater treatment plants.

36. Clean water leaving a treatment plant is called _____.

37. Dirty water entering a treatment plant is called _____.

38. Pump stations are also called _____ stations.

39. The chemical often used to kill germs is _____.

40. Processed sludge that can be used as fertilizer is called _____.

41. Wastewater from toilets is called _____.

42. Wastewater from sinks and showers is called _____.

43. The measure of how acidic or basic water is called _____.

44. Special _____ light can kill germs without chemicals.

45. The nutrient that can cause algae problems is _____.

46. Another name for a settling tank is a _____.

47. The process where particles stick together is called _____.

48. Large shallow ponds used for treatment are called _____.

49. The pipe where clean water flows back to nature is called an _____.

50. Harmful germs that can make people sick are called _____.

51. Gravity helps water flow through sewer pipes. _____

52. Primary treatment removes the tiniest particles from wastewater. _____

53. Bacteria in wastewater treatment are helpful organisms. _____

54. Screening uses metal grids that work like giant strainers. _____

55. All sludge from treatment plants must be thrown away. _____

56. Pump stations are only needed when water flows downhill. _____

57. Secondary treatment uses bacteria to eat remaining waste. _____

58. Chlorine is the only way to disinfect water. _____

59. Civil engineers determine the size needed for treatment plants. _____

60. Wastewater only comes from homes. _____

61. The clean water cycle helps water get used over and over again. _____

62. Grit removal happens after primary clarification. _____

63. Aeration adds oxygen to help bacteria grow. _____

64. Blackwater is cleaner than greywater. _____

65. Environmental engineers specialize in protecting the environment. _____

66. Water quality technicians test water samples throughout treatment. _____

67. All treatment plants are the same size. _____

68. Disinfection is the first step in wastewater treatment. _____

69. Treated wastewater can be safely released back to nature. _____

70. pH measures the temperature of water. _____

Quiz Answer Key

Multiple Choice	Fill-in-the-Blank	True/False
1. b	26. wastewater	51. True
2. c	27. sewer	52. False
3. b	28. screening	53. True
4. a	29. grit	54. True
5. c	30. aeration	55. False
6. c	31. scum	56. False
7. d	32. sludge	57. True
8. b	33. bacteria	58. False
9. c	34. disinfection	59. True
10. d	35. civil	60. False
11. b	36. effluent	61. True
12. c	37. influent	62. False
13. c	38. lift	63. True
14. b	39. chlorine	64. False
15. d	40. biosolids	65. True
16. b	41. blackwater	66. True
17. c	42. greywater	67. False
18. b	43. pH	68. False
19. c	44. ultraviolet (or UV)	69. True
20. b	45. phosphorus	70. False
21. c	46. clarifier	
22. c	47. coagulation	
23. d	48. lagoons	
24. b	49. outfall	
25. c	50. pathogens	

Take a look at other subjects Lila and Andy are learning about...

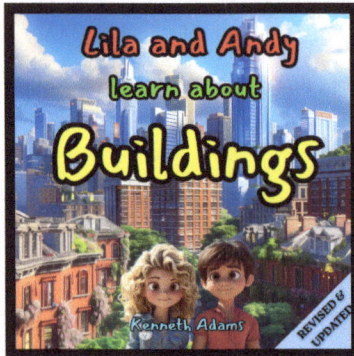

Lila and Andy learn about **Buildings** — Kenneth Adams

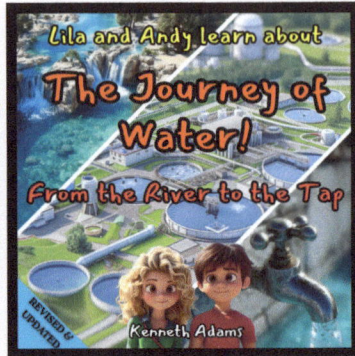

Lila and Andy learn about **The Journey of Water!** From the River to the Tap — Kenneth Adams

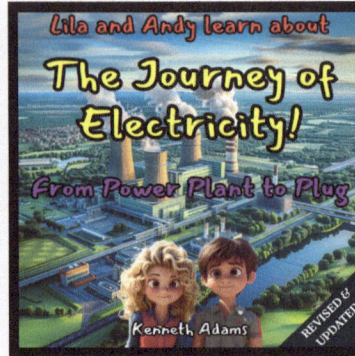

Lila and Andy learn about **The Journey of Electricity!** From Power Plant to Plug — Kenneth Adams

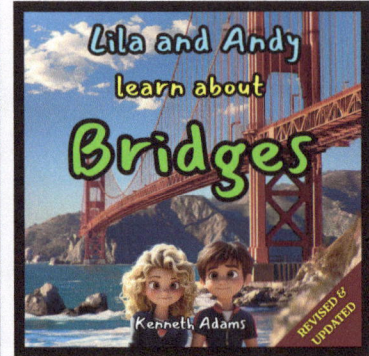

Lila and Andy learn about **Bridges** — Kenneth Adams

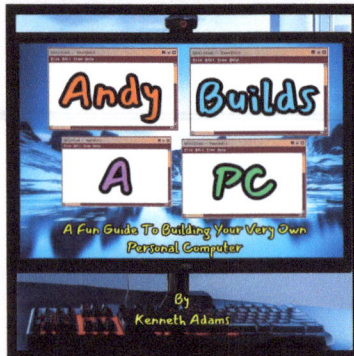

Andy Builds A PC — A Fun Guide To Building Your Very Own Personal Computer — By Kenneth Adams

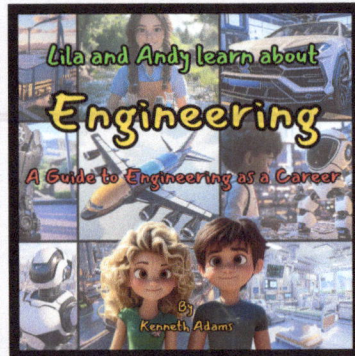

Lila and Andy learn about **Engineering** — A Guide to Engineering as a Career — Kenneth Adams

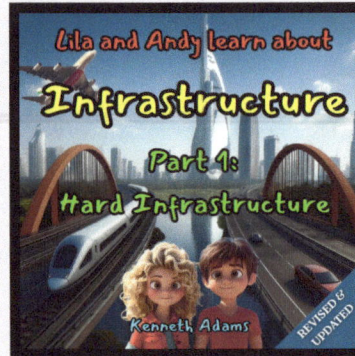

Lila and Andy learn about **Infrastructure** Part 1: Hard Infrastructure — Kenneth Adams

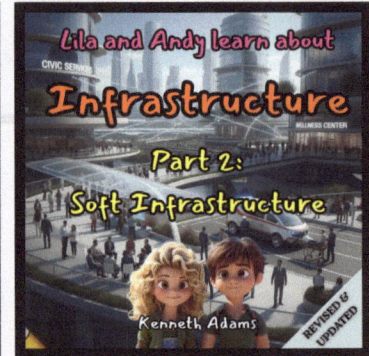

Lila and Andy learn about **Infrastructure** Part 2: Soft Infrastructure — Kenneth Adams

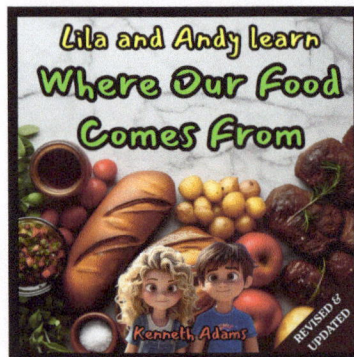

Lila and Andy learn **Where Our Food Comes From** — Kenneth Adams

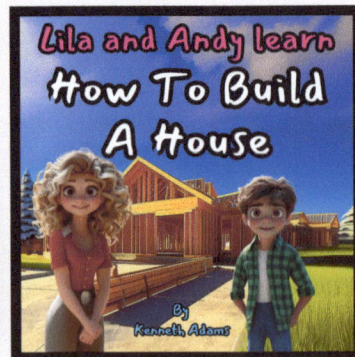

Lila and Andy learn **How To Build A House** — By Kenneth Adams

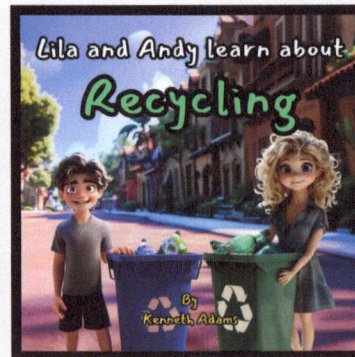

Lila and Andy learn about **Recycling** — By Kenneth Adams

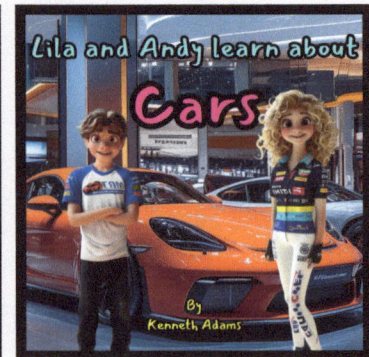

Lila and Andy learn about **Cars** — By Kenneth Adams

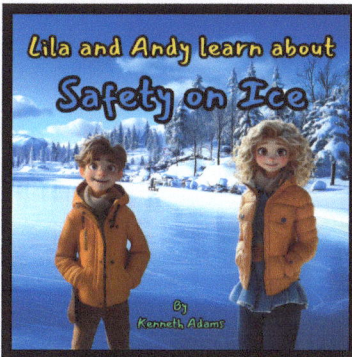
Lila and Andy learn about **Safety on Ice**
By Kenneth Adams

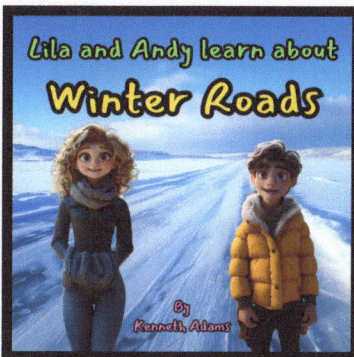
Lila and Andy learn about **Winter Roads**
By Kenneth Adams

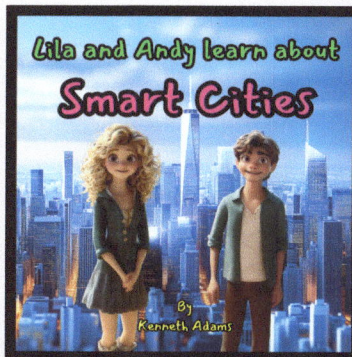
Lila and Andy learn about **Smart Cities**
By Kenneth Adams

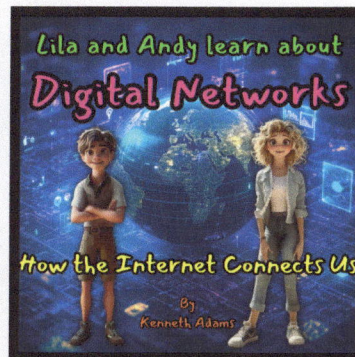
Lila and Andy learn about **Digital Networks**
How the Internet Connects Us
By Kenneth Adams

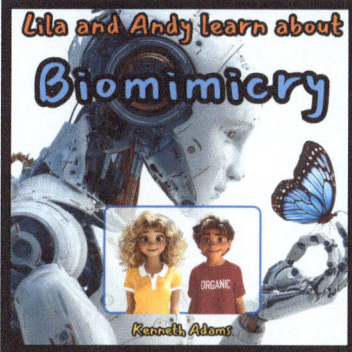
Lila and Andy learn about **Biomimicry**
Kenneth Adams

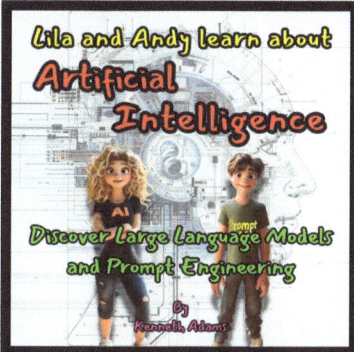
Lila and Andy learn about **Artificial Intelligence**
Discover Large Language Models and Prompt Engineering
By Kenneth Adams

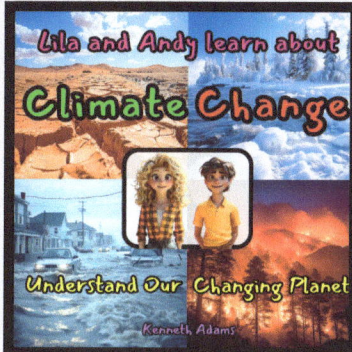
Lila and Andy learn about **Climate Change**
Understand Our Changing Planet
Kenneth Adams

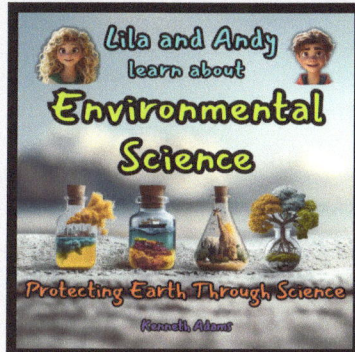
Lila and Andy learn about **Environmental Science**
Protecting Earth Through Science
Kenneth Adams

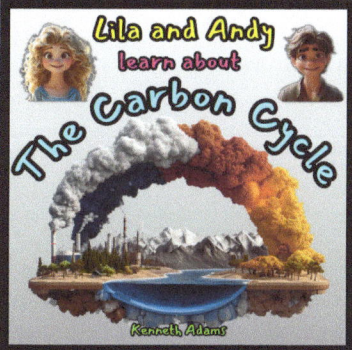
Lila and Andy learn about **The Carbon Cycle**
Kenneth Adams

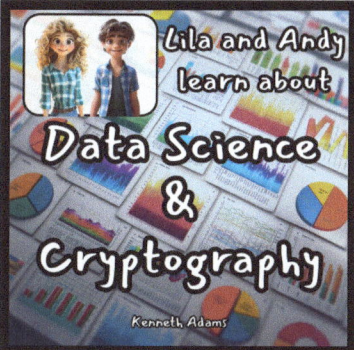
Lila and Andy learn about **Data Science & Cryptography**
Kenneth Adams

Available on Amazon.

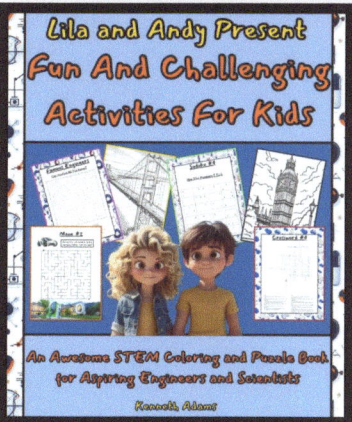
Lila and Andy Present **Fun And Challenging Activities For Kids**
An Awesome STEM Coloring and Puzzle Book for Aspiring Engineers and Scientists
Kenneth Adams

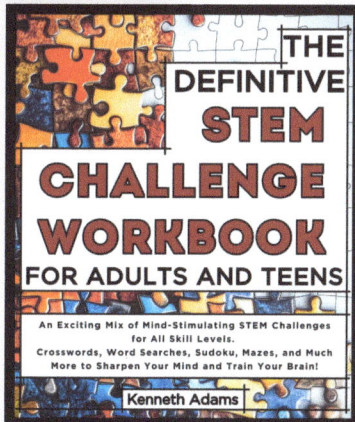
THE DEFINITIVE STEM CHALLENGE WORKBOOK FOR ADULTS AND TEENS
An Exciting Mix of Mind-Stimulating STEM Challenges for All Skill Levels.
Crosswords, Word Searches, Sudoku, Mazes, and Much More to Sharpen Your Mind and Train Your Brain!
Kenneth Adams

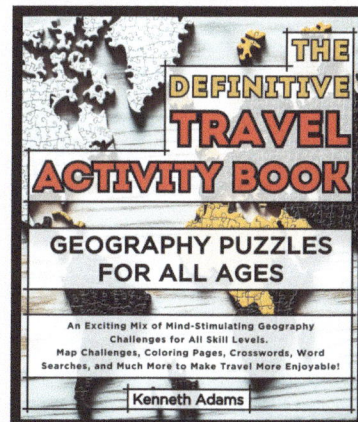
THE DEFINITIVE TRAVEL ACTIVITY BOOK
GEOGRAPHY PUZZLES FOR ALL AGES
An Exciting Mix of Mind-Stimulating Geography Challenges for All Skill Levels.
Map Challenges, Coloring Pages, Crosswords, Word Searches, and Much More to Make Travel More Enjoyable!
Kenneth Adams

www.ingramcontent.com/pod-product-compliance
Lightning Source LLC
Chambersburg PA
CBHW040916100426
42737CB00042B/93